A Little Book of
Scotch Whiskies

Derek Cooper

ILLUSTRATED BY JANE DODDS

Chronicle Books

First published in 1992 by
The Appletree Press Ltd,
7 James Street South, Belfast BT2 8DL.
Copyright © 1992 The Appletree Press, Ltd.
Illustrations © 1992 The Appletree Press, Ltd.
Printed in the E. C. All rights reserved.
No part of this publication may be reproduced
or transmitted in any form or by means,
electronic or mechanical, photocopying,
recording or any information and retrieval
system, without permission in writing from
the publisher.

A Little Book of Scotch Whiskies

First published in the United States in 1992 by
Chronicle Books, 275 Fifth street,
San Francisco, CA 94103

ISBN 0-8118-0253-1

9 8 7 6 5 4 3 2 1

Introduction

For decades, most of the magnificent malt whiskies distilled in Scotland have disappeared into blends; that is, they were married to grain whiskies and sold as 'Scotch'.

The recent revival of interest in single malt whiskies has led to a remarkable demand for them. Societies have been formed to discuss their virtues; tastings are held worldwide at which connoisseurs discourse learnedly on the history of malts, their provenance, and the factors that makes each one of them so individual.

The unique character of these malts derives, not only from the barley and the water, but from the skill of generations of maltsters and distillers whose expertise in the production of *uisge beatha* — the water of life — dates back to the eighteenth century and beyond.

There is a malt for every occasion from the light and fragrant aperitif dram calculated to set the gastric juices flowing to the classic postprandial whiskies worthy of profound contemplation.

The following pages are designed to unravel the mysteries of one of the world's greatest drinks.

Derek Cooper
Portree, Isle of Skye
1992

In Scotland which abounds with lakes and inlets of the sea and high mountains that occasion frequent rains, the moderate use of Spirituous Liquors has been reckoned cherishing and in some degree necessary.

Seafield Mss 1751

· The Early Days ·

The making of whisky in Scotland descends from two very different traditions — the legal and the clandestine. History is vague about how it started. There are records of distillation in Scotland dating from the fifteenth century. In the early days, its production was linked to monastic orders; the spirit, often compounded with herbs and aromatic spices, was used for medicinal purposes. It was known as *aqua vitae*, the water of life, or in Gaelic, *uisge beatha*. *Uisge* (pronounced *ooshka*) was in time anglicised to *whisky*.

At the beginning of the sixteenth century the Guild of Surgeon Barbers was given the exclusive right to distillation in Edinburgh. By the end of the century so much *uisge* was being produced in rural areas that there was a shortage of barley for making bread and bannocks.

In the middle of the seventeenth century the first tax was levied on whisky and this stimulated illegal distillation. Soon ten times more spirit was being made by enterprising freebooters than by the licensed distillers. In remote areas of the Highlands and Islands, far from the prying eyes of the Revenue officers, carefully hidden stills turned out illicit whisky which was smuggled south to the large towns. Many a farmhouse had its private still where surplus barley could be converted into casks of *uisge* not only for home consumption but for use as a valuable liquid currency.

It wasn't until 1823 when the Excise Act made illicit production less profitable that smuggling began to decline. Scores of illegal whisky-makers bought licences and acquired respectability — the great whisky boom was about to begin.

4

· The Making of It ·

The making is deceptively simple. You take barley malt, ferment it, distil it, age it and then drink it.

Barley

Barley has been grown in Scotland since prehistoric times. It used to be called *bigg* or *bere*. Small quantities of *bere* are still grown on the island of Orkney for making beremeal bannocks. Modern strains of barley are preferred for whisky-making, however; they are full of starch and low in protein.

Malting

To convert its starch into soluble sugars, barley is first of all steeped in water and then allowed to sprout or germinate. This used to be done by spreading the wet barley out on malting floors but these days mechanised maltings have largely taken over. At a certain stage sprouting is terminated by drying the green malt. Traditionally, this was done in kilns over peat fires and the peat reek imparted to whisky its pungent and smoky flavour. A proportion of peat is still used at the drying stage. Some malt is markedly peaty, some is only mildly peated. The degree of peating can be tasted in the glass.

To listen to the silence of five thousand casks of whisky in the twilight of a warehouse while the barley seed is being scattered on the surrounding fields might make even a Poet Laureate dumb.

Neil Gunn

Crushing

When the malt is ready for distilling it is ground in a small mill which crushes the grains to produce a rough meal or flour known as *grist*.

Fermenting

The grist is placed in circular mash tuns and covered with water warmed to about 64°C which encourages the enzymes in the malt to convert the starch into sugar. At this stage the mash looks like a thin gruel. The liquid which comes off is known as *wort*. The wort is cooled and pumped into washbacks where yeast is added. A violent fermentation converts the sugar into alcohol and the final liquid is known as *wash*.

Distilling

The wash is then boiled in the wash still and condensed into a concentrated form known as *low wines*. The low wines are distilled for a second time in the spirit still and from this a condensation of spirit is collected which will in time become whisky. In a handful of distilleries three distillations are required before potable spirit is produced.

> Moderation sir, aye, moderation is my rule. Nine or ten is reasonable refreshment, but after that it's apt to degenerate into drinking.
>
> *Old Man in a Highland Tavern*

Maturation

The spirit which finally comes off the still and is collected in the spirit receiver cannot legally be described as whisky until t has been matured in oak casks for a minimum of three years. During maturation the whisky undergoes a lengthy period of refinement in which it mellows and reaches its optimum quality.

Strength

Whisky comes from the still at a fiery strength which varies between 60 to 75 percentage of alcohol. Before filling it into casks, the spirit is "reduced" with spring water to an average strength of 65% alcohol and, during the years in wood a proportion of the alcohol will be lost, further diminishing its strength. Most single malts are once again reduced before bottling and marketed at 40% alcohol which is roughly equivalent to the old proof strength of 70% alcohol. In Britain, duty or tax paid to the exchequer is based on strength: the stronger the whisky the more the tax.

· The Influences on Malt Whisky ·

Water

No distillery can operate without limitless supplies of water. Pure spring water is needed for steeping the barley, mashing the malt, and reducing the raw spirit to bring it down to a suitable strength for aging. Cold water is also needed to cool the coils in which the vaporised contents of the still are condensed into liquid spirit.

Some say that the best kind of spring water rises from granite and flows over peat. Most Scottish water is 'soft' although there are exceptions; for example, the springs which make Glenmorangie have a very high calcium content and are rich in minerals.

Stills

All malt whisky stills are beaten from copper and are onion-shaped. They are really giant kettles in which the wash is heated to the point where the alcohol (which has a lower boiling point than water) is driven off and, rising into a worm-shaped tube which is constantly cooled by water, is then condensed into liquid spirit.

In the old days, stills were heated over peat or coal fires. Today, most stills are fuelled by gas or oil. The angle of the lyne arm — the pipe which connects the head of the still to the condensing unit — affects the style of the spirit. So does the shape of the still, the degree and fierceness of the heat applied to the wash, and the skill with which the potable part of the distillation is collected. Generally, tall stills produce light whiskies, stills with short necks produce heavier whiskies.

Wood

After distilling and reduction with spring water to the strength which the individual distillery favours, the spirit is "filled" into oak hogsheads and butts where it will be left to mature for sometimes up to 50 years. The optimum age of a malt varies. Many are excellent at 5 or 8 years; others are given much longer maturation. Most malt whisky is aged in

merican casks which have previously been used in the USA to hold Bourbon whiskey. Sherry casks are eagerly sought ter. When sherry was exported to Britain in wooden casks ost of these, when empty, were sold on to the distilleries. ewer sherry casks are available these days and distilleries like acallan, which mature all their spirit in sherry casks, buy em in Jerez.

Most distilleries use a mix of casks: some American oak, ome sherry oak. Sherry wood imparts a rich depth and colour o the spirit; the influence of casks previously used for ourbon is less egregious. During maturation, oxidation and vaporation remove the harsher elements which are noticeable spirit straight from the still and the whisky gradually loses rength. The smaller the cask, the sooner the whisky atures.

limate

ost distillers believe that they produce better whisky in the old winter months than in the heat of summer. There are xperts who claim to be able to detect the difference etween a cask filled in January and one from a September stillation. The humidity and temperature of the warehouses which the casks lie also influence the maturing of the hisky. Casks stored near the sea *may* well have a tang of zone about them — but you may find that fanciful.

The most important ingredient in malt whisky is the people who make it.

Jim McEwan, Manager of Bowmore

· Geography ·

It has been customary to divide whiskies into geographic regions according to where they are made. A useful distinction is between Lowland and Highland malts.

Lowland

These malts are made south of the imaginary line drawn from Greenock on the west coast of Scotland to Dundee on the east. They tend to be lighter and softer and less heavily peated than some of the whiskies produced north of the Highland line. Names to note are: Auchentoshan, Bladnoch, Rosebank, Littlemill, Glenkinchie.

Highland

The highland malts are renowned for their strong character, their classic depth and idiosyncratic complexity. The majority of distilleries in the Highlands are located in rural surroundings usually on the banks of streams and burns and more often than not surrounded by areas of great natural beauty. They fall naturally into the following sub-divisions:

Speyside

This is the heartland of malt whisky distilling. Well over half of the country's distilleries are found here clustered round such rivers as the Findhorn, Lossie, Livet, Deveron, Fiddich, Dullan and the glorious Spey itself which runs a hundred miles from the wilds of Badenoch north to Spey Bay on the Moray coast. The greatest whiskies of all come from Speyside: Strathisla, Aultmore, Dufftown, Mortlach, Glenfiddich,

HIGHLAND PARK

SINGLE MALT SCOTCH WHISKY

ORKNEY ✦ ISLANDS

PRODUCT OF SCOTLAND

Glenlivet, Glenfarclas, Macallan, Aberlour, Balmenach, Cardhu, Knockando, Glen Grant, Tamdhu — the congregation of historic and distinguished malts is remarkable.

The North

A smaller roll call of great names here but they include Highland Park and Scapa on mainland Orkney, and the coastal distilleries of Glenmorangie, Pulteney, Balblair, Clynelish and Dalmore.

The East

Aberdeenshire was once a centre of feverish smuggling and around the eastern seaboard there are many distinguished malts: Glengarioch at Old Meldrum, Lochnagar near Balmoral, Fettercairn, Glendronach at Forgue, and Glenglassaugh in Portsoy which is also famous for its marble.

The West

Only a small handful of distilleries are left here of which Glengoyne, just 12 miles north of Glasgow, is the most notable. Oban is proud of its local distillery which was founded in the eighteenth century. Further north, Fort William has had a famous distillery called Ben Nevis since 1825. The islands of Mull, Jura and Skye each have one distillery: Tobermory, Jura, and Talisker, respectively.

Islay

This windswept and often gale-lashed island due west of Glasgow produces some of the great classic malts. These 8 distilleries make whiskies which are remarkable for their pungency and their subtly-different flavour profiles. At the majestic end of the scale are the full and oily Laphroaig and the powerful peaty Lagavulin; at the other end are the lighter Bruichladdich and the delicate Bunnahabhainn.

Campbeltown

At one time there were just over 20 distilleries in this, the largest town in Kintyre. Its full-flavoured malts were in constant demand for blending with grain whiskies. Only two distilleries survive: Glen Scotia, which dates from 1832, and Springbank, which dates from 1828.

· The Enjoyment of Malt Whisky ·

Thirty years ago most single malt whiskies were difficult to buy outside Scotland except in specialist wine and spirit merchants. The Victorians believed that the best way to drink malt whisky was in a blend with the blander grain whiskies. These blended whiskies with internationally-known names like Haig, Dewar, Bell's, Johnnie Walker, White Horse and Teacher's dominated the market. As post war whisky drinkers became more interested in what went into "Scotch" they began to demand malt whiskies in their single state. Like the châteaux of Bordeaux, the distilleries of Scotland began to achieve a fame they had been denied since the 1860s when the rise of blending buried their individual virtues in anonymity and soda water drowned their unique qualities. Today, almost all distilleries bottle a small proportion of their output in the single state while other distilleries — Macallan, Glenfiddich, Glenmorangie and Balvenie, for instance — reserve most or all of their whisky for sale as single malts.

Tasting

Although blended whiskies have been traditionally served on the rocks or mixed with soda water or ginger ale, malt

hiskies deserve more sensitive treatment. Once whisky is
ottled it does not go on maturing so there is nothing to be
ained in "laying it down" as one would with port or claret.
alt whisky should be served at room temperature in a glass
hich will enable you to appreciate its colour and appraise its
ouquet.

Some of the heavier more magisterial malts are best
njoyed in the manner of cognac or armagnac in an undiluted
ate as an after-dinner digestif. Others release their aromas
illingly when a little spring water is added to the glass — not
oda water or tap water but the purest spring or branch
ater you can obtain.

Scotland has it in its power to give the world such
whisky as few can dream of. Léoville, Margaux and
Latour might be matched with Islay, Glenfiddich and
Glen Grant. Haut Brion singing aloud might hear in reply
the *voix d'or* of Highland Park and the brown steams of
Glenlivet would need not envy the sun-warmed slopes
of Bordeaux.

Eric Linklater, 1935

en Light Aperitif Malts

adnoch, Littlemill, Tobermory, Port Ellen, Glenkinchie,
eanston, Glenury-Royal, Glen Keith, Dalwhinnie, Teaninich.

en Weightier Digestif Malts

berlour, Convalmore, Dailuaine, Glendronach, Miltonduff,
almore, Glencadam, Speyburn, Auchroisk, Laphroaig.

· Malt Whisky – The Language ·

Single Malts

These are the product of a distillery whose name they bea
Before bottling, a selection of casks distilled in differe
months and years will be married together. If an age
declared on the label, that age will refer not to the olde
whisky in the batch but the youngest — thus an 8-year-c
bottle may well contain older whiskies. Some labels decla
the year of distillation but, since aging ceases on bottling, th
is not very helpful unless the year of bottling is also giver

Vatted Malts

These are malt whiskies from various distilleries which hav
been married or "vatted" together to produce a harmonio
whole. The distilleries from which the whiskies come are no
generally named. Examples are Glenleven, Mar Lodge, Roy
Culross, Glen Drummond and Glencoe. Gordon and Macph
of Elgin sell a quartet of 12-year-old vatted malts which the
call Pride of the Lowlands, Pride of Strathspey, Pride of Isla
and Pride of Orkney, all designed to reflect the essenti
character of those areas.

Very often a distillery will find in their warehouses a sm
parcel of malts of unusual interest either because of their ag
or their quality and these will be bottled in small amounts ar
sold for high prices. Such malts are eagerly collected !
connoisseurs.

The Scotch Malt Whisky Society, which has 10,000 membe
bottles single cask malts at cask strength and avoids chil

ltering them, a process which the industry has adopted to prevent diluted whisky from going cloudy at low temperatures. Sadly, the filtering removes many of the impurities which contribute so much to the personality of malt whisky. The Society's bottlings are therefore eagerly sought after.

Thanks to the growing interest in well-aged malts it is now possible to have comparative tastings of outstanding malts at various stages of development. Glenfarclas, for instance, can currently be acquired at 8, 10, 12, 15, 18, 21 and 25 years old. Recently a bottle of a 60-year-old example of The Macallan fetched £6000.

· Distilleries ·

Visiting

Due to the recession of the 1980s some famous distilleries have closed their doors. Some, alas, like Glen Mhor and Glen Albyn in Inverness and Banff, which was built in 1824, have been demolished; others, such as Glenugie, have been sold for other uses. St Magdalene in Linlithgow has been converted into flats and Dallas Dhu is now a museum run by the Scottish Historic Buildings directorate. However, just under 90 survive, of which some 70 either have reception centres or are happy to welcome visitors. As well as Dallas Dhu, which is full of interest, enthusiasts will find plenty to see at the Cairngorm Whisky Centre, the Museum in Aviemore, and the Scotch Whisky Heritage Centre on Edinburgh's Royal Mile.

· Distilleries Currently Working ·

Aberfeldy, Aberlour, Allt a Bhainne, Ardbeg, Ardmor
Auchentoshan, Auchroisk, Aultmore, Balblair, Balmenac
Balvenie, Benrinnes, Bladnoch, Blair Athol, Bowmore, Brack
Braes of Glenlivet, Bruichladdich, Bunnahabhainn, Caol Il
Caperdonich, Cardhu, Clynelish, Cragganmore, Craigellachi
Dailuaine, Dalmore, Dalwhinnie, Dufftown, Edradou
Fettercairn, Glenburgie, Glencadam, Glendronach, Glendulla
Glen Elgin, Glenesk, Glenfarclas, Glenfiddich, Glen Garioc
Glengoyne, Glen Grant, Glen Keith, Glenkinchie, Glenlive
Glenlossie, Glenmorangie, Glen Moray, Glenordie, Glenrothe
Glen Scotia, Glen Spey, Glentauchers, Glenturret, Highlan
Park, Inchgower, Inverleven, Jura, Knockando, Knockdh
Lagavulin, Laphroaig, Linkwood, Littlemill, Lochnagar, Lochsid
Longmorn, Macallan, Macduff, Miltonduff, Mortlach, Oba
Pulteney, Rosebank, Scapa, Speyburn, Springbank, Strathisl
Talisker, Tamdhu, Tamnavulin, Tobermory, Tomati
Tomintoul, Tormore, Tullibardine.

A clergyman was administering consolation to a
dying Highlander when he was shocked by the old man
asking if there was any whisky in heaven. Half
apologetically he added, "Ye ken, sir, it's not that I care
for it, but it looks well on the table."

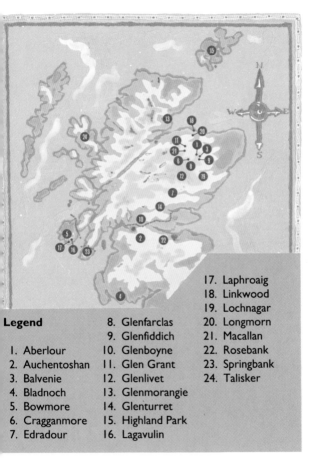

Legend

1. Aberlour
2. Auchentoshan
3. Balvenie
4. Bladnoch
5. Bowmore
6. Cragganmore
7. Edradour
8. Glenfarclas
9. Glenfiddich
10. Glenboyne
11. Glen Grant
12. Glenlivet
13. Glenmorangie
14. Glenturret
15. Highland Park
16. Lagavulin
17. Laphroaig
18. Linkwood
19. Lochnagar
20. Longmorn
21. Macallan
22. Rosebank
23. Springbank
24. Talisker

· Twenty Four Distilleries ·

Aberlour

The first distillery was built in the village of Aberlour in 1826. Renovated in 1880, it lies in the shadow of Ben Rinnes on the banks of the Lour burn close to where it joins the rushing waters of the Spey; in Victorian times the entire operation was run by waterpower. The waters for mashing the malt come from the famous well dedicated to St. Drostan which stands in the distillery grounds. Sold at 10 and 12 years old, Aberlour is smooth and soft with subdued sherry and malt tones: a gentle digestif whisky.

Auchentoshan

Auchentoshan, on the outskirts of Glasgow, was founded in 1825. The whisky is triple-distilled, a once-common practice in the Lowlands. Although the distillery is located south of the mythical "Highland Line", it draws its water from Loch Cochno, thus making it the only Lowland whisky to be made with Highland water. Lightly peated, gold in colour, Auchentoshan is a gentle flowery malt with a perceptible sweetness.

Whisky to a Scotchman is as innocent as milk is to the rest of the human race.

Mark Twain

Balvenie

Built in 1892 by William Grant, the owner of Glenfiddich, Balvenie sits lower down the hill on the same site. It draws its water from the same spring, takes its name from the castle in whose shadow it lies, and continues to malt a proportion of its barley on traditional floor maltings. The whisky it produces in its four wash and four spirit stills is a heavy, honeyed, beautifully-balanced after-dinner malt marketed in a distinctive long-necked bottle.

Bladnoch

On the banks of the river Bladnoch, a mile from Wigtown, sits the most southerly of all Scotland's distilleries. Built in 1817, enlarged in 1978, renovated in 1957 and again in 1965, Bladnoch is small, using only a pair of stills but its whisky is highly prized by connoisseurs of Lowland malts. A light spirit with unexpected fullness in the finish, it can be drunk either as an aperitif or a digestif.

Whisky is a mystery, a magic of locality. The foreigner may import not only Scottish barley, but Scottish water, Scottish distilling apparatus and set a Scot to work on them, but the glory evaporates: it will not travel.

Ivor Brown

MORRISON'S

BOWMORE

ISLAY

ISLAY

Single Malt

SCOTCH WHISKY

Years **10** Old

DISTILLED AND BOTTLED IN SCOTLAND

Bowmore

is distillery was established in 1779 making it the oldest in
ay and one of the oldest in the country. Its reception centre
mmands beautiful sea views. Like Balvenie, the distillery
tains its old-fashioned floor maltings. One of the most
mplex whiskies of all, Bowmore has hints of peatsmoke,
ather, seaspray and a fleeting fruitiness. It attains a majesty
hich reflects two centuries of continuous production.

Cragganmore

ing at Ballindalloch in the heart of the mountains close to
e Spey, this distillery was built on the site of a smuggling
thy in 1869. It draws its water from the Craggan hill springs.
s four tall stills produce a greatly underestimated spirit with
remarkable ability to age gracefully. For some years I
ssessed a bottle distilled in 1925 and its remarkable aromas
ger powerfully in the memory. It had all the virtues of an
d cognac coupled with the whole spectrum of flavours
culiar to malted barley.

> Then let us toast John Barleycorn,
> Each man a glass in hand,
> And may his great prosperity
> Ne'er fail in old Scotland
>
> *Robert Burns, 1787*

Edradour

This is the smallest and most picturesquely-sited distillery all. At one time a farm, it sits in a Perthshire glen ne Pitlochry through which flows a tumbling burn. Built in 182 the distillery now has an absorbing new visitor centre but remains unspoilt and is full of early nineteenth century bucol charm. The malt is unusually dry, smooth, sherried and frui — a model whisky from a model distillery.

Glenfarclas

The distillery was built in 1836 and stands isolated on tl moors at the foot of Ben Rinnes where the Avon joins tl Spey. There is a fine visitor centre which is lined with o panelling rescued from the liner *S.S. Australia*. The famil owned distillery supports a farm and a herd of prize-winni Aberdeen Angus cattle. Its stills, the largest on Speysid produce a malt which is available in a range of ages from 8 25 years old. Matured in sherry casks, the spirit is bi generous, and possessed of a huge bouquet and a long fragra finish.

> This is smart stuff.
> *John Keats on tasting whis,*
> *for the first time in 18,*

Glenfiddich

In 1886 William Grant invested his entire capital of £775 in constructing this now internationally-renowned distillery which has the smallest stills — 29 of them — in Scotland. The original malt barn was converted into a visitor centre in 1869 and 100,000 tourists pass through it every year. Glenfiddich was the first distillery to create a world market for single malt whisky and today it remains the biggest selling malt of all. Easy to appreciate, this is a carefully-balanced dram for all occasions.

> Lord grant guid luck tae' a' the Grants
> Likewise eternal bliss,
> For they should sit among the Sa'nts
> That make a dram like this.
> *Lines beneath the founder's portrait in the London office*

Glengoyne

Built in 1833 at the foot of Dungoyne 12 miles from Glasgow, the distillery lies in a pretty little glen with a dashing waterfall at its head. The distillery, and the warehouses on the other side of the road, lie on the Highland Line but Lang Brothers who own Glengoyne are firmly of the opinion that it has all the enviable characteristics of a Highland malt. Fruity and smooth, a proportion of the spirit is matured in sherry casks. Sold at 10, 12 and 17 years old, it is a discreet and light whisky which is winning more admirers every year.

Glen Grant

Major James Grant built his distillery in the village of Rothes in 1840 and in due course it became the first works in Scotland to have the then new-fangled electricity. For over 90 years Glen Grant has been the best-selling malt in Scotland and, internationally, it now rivals Glenfiddich. It's one of the classic malts — flowery, full of fruit and aging effortlessly. The 24-year-old malt is strongly sherried and full of Highland character

The Glenlivet

So historic and hallowed that it carries its own very definite article, The Glenlivet is unarguably the most famous, if not the greatest, whisky in the world. Originally licensed in 1824 by a former smuggler called George Smith, the present distillery, which dates from 1858, is set on the moors of Minmore and produces the king of whiskies: full-bodied, subtly-peated, delicate, mellow, aromatic and immensely self-confident. A remarkable malt.

> Gie me the real Glenlivet ... the human mind never tires o' Glenlivet. If a body could just find oot the exac' proportion and quantity that ought to be drunk every day, and keep to that, I verily trow that he might leeve for ever, without dying at a', and that doctors and kirkyards would go oot o' fashion.
>
> *James Hogg, 1827*

Glenmorangie

Glenmorangie (with the stress on the second syllable) is sited on the edge of the Dornoch Firth at Tain. Its four stills are the tallest of any in Scotland. Self-coloured, lightly-peated, matured in American Bourbon casks in earth-floored warehouses and made from hard water which bubbles out of the ground into a small crystal clean pool in the Tarlogie Hills, Glenmorangie is one of the finest malts available. Soft, flowery and fragrant, it is the restrained ideal to which many lesser spirits would dearly love to aspire.

Glenturret

Originally established in 1775, the distillery is set on the banks of the Turret two miles north of Crieff in what was in former times a favoured place for illicit distillation. The elaborate award-winning Heritage centre which is now part of this, the second smallest distillery in Scotland, makes Glenturret a magnet for summer visitors. The malt, mashed, fermented and distilled by a staff of two and sold at various ages from 8 years to 21, is markedly sherried in maturity; full, smooth and deep in flavour.

A fine pot still whisky is as noble a product of Scotland as any burgundy or champagne is of France.

Neil Gunn, 1935

Highland Park

Scotland's most northern distillery lies on the southern outskirts of the Orkney capital of Kirkwall. Its official history is recorded as beginning in 1798 although, like many other distilleries, its roots lie deep in the early lawless smuggling community. Although the barley comes from the mainland, it is malted and dried over locally cut peat. A smoky, dry, enormously imposing malt, Highland Park is one of the most impressive and elegant.

Lagavulin

Like all the Islay distilleries, Lagavulin was built on the coast to make it more accessible to the boats which serviced it and took the casks away. Built in 1816 on the site of a clandestine smugglers' hideaway, Lagavulin preserves its traditional feel and its four stills produce one of the most pungent of all Scottish whiskies. Deep in colour, powerful, assertively peated, smoky, dry, Lagavulin encompasses all the virtues of an historic and classic malt.

> From the bonny bells of heather
> They brewed a drink long-syne,
> Was sweeter far than honey,
> Was stronger far than wine
> *Robert Louis Stevenson (1850–1894)*

Laphroaig

so built on the edge of the sea, a mile from Port Ellen, this
ay distillery produces a whisky which arouses controversial
actions. Although it has become less wild in recent years,
s strongly phenolic, peaty, seaweedy aroma does not appeal
 everyone. In Prohibition days, when whisky in the USA
uld only be obtained in prescription, its medicinal bouquet
osted sales gratifyingly. The distillery was built in 1815 and
tains its floor maltings and kiln. Here the green malt is dried
er aromatic peat cut from the company's own peat moors
 be distilled into one of the most interesting and challenging
alts of all.

Linkwood

e Brown family of Linkwood estate commissioned this
stillery to be built in 1821 to the south of Elgin. Much
novated in 1972, the buildings retain an atmospheric air with
eed-eating swans gliding over the cooling reservoir fed with
ater from the Burn of Linkwood. A high scorer in blind
stings, Linkwood has a cleanness about it which qualifies its
arm sweetness and long-lasting dry finish. A perfect
eyside malt.

Royal Lochnagar

Located in the backyard of the Balmoral estate, Roy
Lochnagar has provided the castle with whisky since the da
of Victoria and Albert. Built in 1826 by John Crathie, an illic
whisky-maker, Lochnagar takes its water from springs whi
rise in the foothills of Lochnagar mountain which is the subje
of a children's story by HRH Prince Charles. The whisky
commanding with a suggestion of smokiness in its mal
depths. John Brown, Queen Victoria's confidante and servar
loved it.

> I have never yet met any blend of all malts that had
> the individuality and distinction of the perfect sample of
> single whisky.
>
> *Neil Gu*

Longmorn

Built in 1894 on the site of a grain mill which had be
operating since the eighteenth century, Longmorn, on th
road between Rothes and Elgin, has 8 stills and is recognis
as producing one of the finest whiskies on Speyside. Like ma
another distillery which has ceased malting its own barle
Longmorn maintains its distinctive kiln with the pagoda roo
A smooth and complex dram, Longmorn is noted for its mult
layered maltiness.

ROYAL LOCHNAGAR

Single Highland Malt

SCOTCH WHISKY

Produced in Scotland

Royal Lochnagar Distillery

CRATHIE, DEESIDE
ABERDEENSHIRE
SCOTLAND

70 cl   40 % Vol

ESTP   1845

BY APPOINTMENT TO THEIR LATE MAJESTIES
QUEEN VICTORIA, KING EDWARD VII & KING GEORGE V

The Macallan

great Speyside malt — some say the greatest — produced in
distillery first licensed in 1824. The 21 small stills, the
sistence on maturing the spirit only in oloroso sherry casks,
e care with which every aspect of the operation is
nducted, have given this prime whisky the title of "the Rolls
yce of single malts" and nobody these days would refer to
with any less courtesy than *The* Macallan. Smooth, soft, dry-
erried, intensely flowery and full of unique character.

Rosebank

though there was a distillery in Falkirk in 1817, the present
ildings date from 1840. There are three stills at Rosebank
d, as at Auchentoshan, triple distillation is practised, a
ocess which creates the light, clean style of whisky for
hich Rosebank is a benchmark. Triple distillation encourages
rly maturity and the 8-year-old whisky is astonishingly
unded and complete; an ideal aperitif.

Whisky-tasting like wine-tasting or tea-tasting is an
art which takes years of study before it can be mastered.
Robert Bruce Lockhart, 1930

Springbank

In the late 1880s there were 21 working distilleries Campbeltown, the seaport capital of the Mull of Kintyr Today, only Springbank and Glen Scotia are distilling. Springba retains its old floor maltings, although they are not current in use, and bottles its spirit at a variety of ages ranging fro 12 to 30 years. Springbank was opened in 1823 and to ent its stone buildings is to step back into the past. Its old sing malts fetch high prices and are eagerly sought in overse markets.

> The King o' drinks, as I conceive it,
> Talisker, Islay or Glenlivet.
> *Robert Louis Stevens*

Talisker

It was Robert Louis Stevenson who described Talisker, fro the misty Isle of Skye, as one of the kings of whisky. Th distillery lies on the shores of Loch Harport with the Alp-lik Cuillin hills rising awesomely on the skyline. After a disastro fire this 1830-built distillery was largely rebuilt in the 1960 It uses heavily-peated malt from the mainland and is splendidly powerful spirit. Drinking it is rather like sippi liquid Harris tweed. A huge malt of great distinction.

· Malt Whisky in the Kitchen ·

Nothing is better for a spartan lunch by the spring on hillside than half a cold grouse with oat-cake and a beaker or two of whisky and water.

Alexander Innes Shand, 1902

The Scots have always regarded whisky not as a culinary ingredient, but as something to be poured down the throat. There is no tradition of using whisky in the kitchen except to cheer up the cook. In recent years, however, inventive chefs have devised a small repertoire of dishes which include fine malts as an ingredient. Ginger and Glenfarclas ice cream, Cragganmore Cranachan, Howtowdie with Highland Park sauce, monkfish poached in The Macallan, herrings potted in Pulteney ... why not? They may lack historical authenticity but they're fun.

Here are three traditional recipes but even they are more for drinking than eating.

Het Pint

This used to be carried in large copper kettles through the streets to welcome in the New Year. This hogmanay brew was mixed from ale, sugar, eggs, grated nutmeg and whisky. Sir Walter Scott described it as an "immemorial libation".

Atholl Brose

This delicious nectar is named after the fifteenth-century Duke of Atholl who is said to have poleaxed his enemy, the Earl of Ross, by doctoring the well at which he was to drink with a lethal mix of oatmeal, heather honey and whisky. Add whipped cream to a dram of malt, sprinkle with lightly toasted oatmeal, serve with shortbread and you have a heady dessert.

Toddy

Sit roun' the table well content
an' steer aboot the toddy.

Of all the rituals associated with whisky none is more civilised than the making of toddy. It is, say many valetudinarians, the perfect specific for a cold: "take your toddy to bed, put one bowler hat at the foot and drink until you see two."

Toddy may well derive its name from Tod's Well which, rising on the slopes of Arthur's Seat, once supplied the citizens of Edinburgh with much of their water. "When it is borne in mind," wrote the poet Allan Ramsay in 1721, "that whisky derives its name from water, it is highly probable that Toddy in like manner was a facetious name for the pure element."

The four partners of the perfect toddy are spring water, sugar lumps, lemon juice (though purists of the old school would regard lemon juice as a blasphemy) and a well matured malt. You need a stout tumbler which must first be warmed with hot water. Then put three or four lumps of sugar in the glass and dissolve them with boiling water. At this stage you may stir in a little lemon juice and top up with your chosen whisky. Then without more ado

> Drink of the stream
> Ere its potency goes
> No bath is refreshing
> Except while it glows

Toddy is a very Scottish elixir which sometimes baffles visitors. Sir Robert Bruce Lockhart, brought up on Speyside, tells the story of a Russian friend who couldn't understand the contrariness of the recipe. "First you put in whisky to make it strong", he said, "then you add water to make it weak. Next you put in lemon to make it sour, then you put in sugar to make it sweet. You put in more whisky to kill the water then you say 'here's to you' – and you drink it yourself!"

• • •

> O Lord, since we have feasted thus
> Which we do little merit
> Let Meg now take away the flesh
> And Jock bring in the spirit
>> *After Grace: Robert Burns at the*
>> *Globe Tavern, Dumfries*

Contents